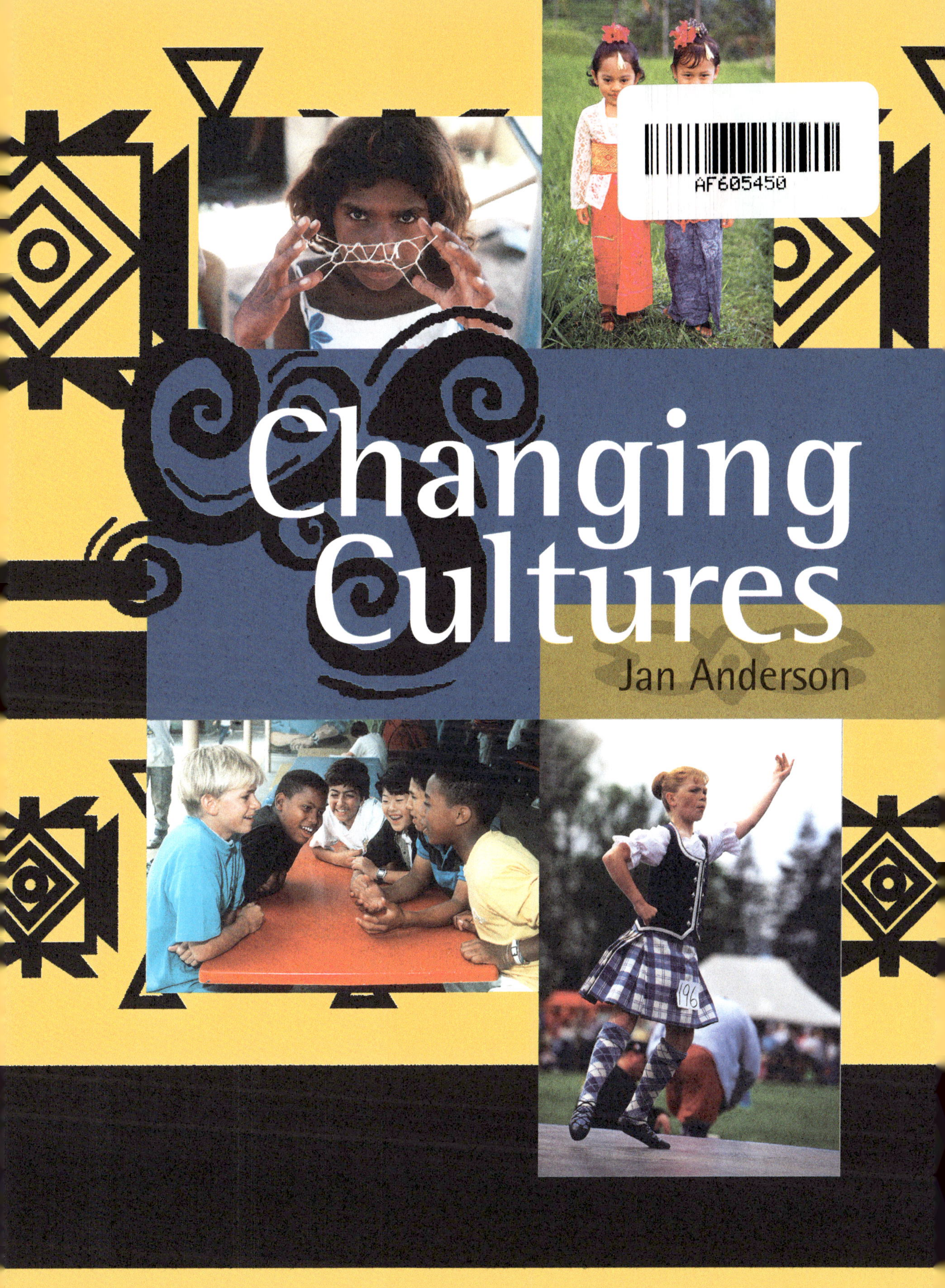

Changing Cultures

Jan Anderson

Changing Cultures

Text: Jan Anderson
Design: Vonda Pestana
Editor: Virginia Gray
Illustrations: Rae Dale
Reprint: Siew Han Ong

Acknowledgements
The author and publisher would like to acknowledge permission to reproduce material from the following sources:
Photographs by AAP Image/AFP/Timothy Clary, p. 22 top /Top Cole, p. 23 bottom;Austral International/Stock Food, pp. 9, 12 top; Australian Picture Library, p. 26; Australian Picture Library/Corbis, pp. 7 bottom, 16 bottom right, 23 top /Ludo Kuipers, front cover top left, p 19 /Galen Rowell, front cover top right, p. 21 top /Brian A. Wikander, front cover bottom left, p. 15 bottom left /Galen Rowell, back cover /Catherin Karnow, p. 8 bottom /David Lees, p, 12bottom /Horan Tom, p. 13/Paul Barton, p. 14 /Jan Butchofsky-Houser, p. 15 top /Adam Woolfitt, p. 16 top left /Judy Griesedieck, p. 16 bottom left /Peter M. Wilson, p. 17 top right /Joyce Choo, p. 18 right /Clay Perry, p. 25 top right /Jim Cumminsl Era Publications for the photograph on p. 29 and extract pp. 29, 30 adapted from MARIA DONATO; When I was Youngl Copyright (c) 1996, Janeen Brian. First Published by Era Publications, Australia; Imagen/Bill Thomas, p.5 top; Lochman Transparancies, p. 7 top; Lonely Planet Images, pp. 4 bottom left, 11 top, 17 top left; Newspix, pp. 27 top & bottom, 28; Nokia, p. 4 bottom right; Photo Japan, p. 8 top; Photo New Zealand, p. 24 bottom left / Sarah Masters, p. 24 bottom right; Photodisc, p. 6 top; PhotoEdit/Marie Kate Denny, front cover bottom right, p.20 top; Photolibrary.com/Foodpix, p.6 bottom /Rick Sherwin, p. 15 bottom right /SuperStock, p. 24 top right; Phtos.com, p. 20 bottoml Stock Photos/Masterfile, p, 21 bottom, p. 24 top left, p. 25 top left.

PM Extras Non-Fiction
Ruby
Caring for the Earth
Changing Cultures
Having Fun, Then and Now
Change in the Community
Communities Everywhere
Past Work, Future Work

For product information and technology assistance,
in Australia call 1300 790 853;
in New Zealand call 0508 635 766

For permission to use material from this text or product,
please email **aust.permissions@cengage.com**

ISBN 978 0 17 011466 0
ISBN 978 0 17 011464 6 (set)

Cengage Learning Australia
Level 7, 80 Dorcas Street
South Melbourne, Victoria Australia 3205

Cengage Learning New Zealand
Unit 4B Rosedale Office Park
331 Rosedale Road, Albany, North Shore NZ 0632

For learning solutions, visit **cengage.com.au**

Printed in Australia by Ligare Pty Ltd
15 16 17 23 22 21

Contents

Where in the World ...

Many of us were born in another country, or have parents and family who come from another part of the world. As both people and products move around the world, they bring far-away cultures closer together.

At home we cook with spices from India, at work we use mobile phones from Finland, and at school there are computers made in Japan or the United States of America.

Spices from India

Learning about other cultures allows us to discover new ways of doing things. We can listen to different kinds of music and enjoy unusual foods.

And we don't have to travel too far. We can explore almost every corner of the globe by using the internet. At the click of a mouse, we can be **virtual travellers**, and find out about cultures in many parts of the world that we've never even seen!

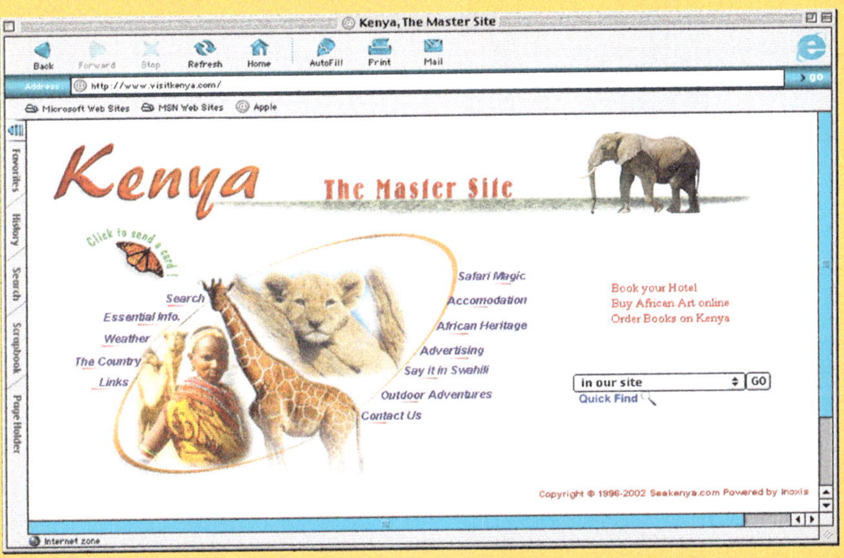

CHAPTER 2

Food

When people **migrate** from one country to another, they often take their recipes and cooking styles with them. Sometimes these migrants, or new settlers, start restaurants. So people living in Paris, New York or Sydney can enjoy the foods of many different cultures all in the one place.

Traditionally, one of Britain's national dishes was roast beef and Yorkshire pudding, but today, an Indian chicken tikka masala is just as common!

Quandongs

Wattle seed

Bush tucker

In Australia, bush **tucker**, or food that has been used by Aborigines for centuries, is now included in some modern Australian recipes.

Quandongs (said kwon-dongs) are a kind of native Australian fruit. They can be dried and preserved for later. Quandongs taste like apricots and can be made into a sweet pie.

Wattle seed is now used in some Australian breads and biscuits. Qantas – the Australian national airline – has served wattle seed bread rolls with meals.

In some places, the tea ceremc is held in a separate 'tea hou set in a beautiful gard

The Japanese Tea Ceremony

The Japanese tea **ceremony** is a tradition that is 800 years old. The ceremony, which can take some time, is meant to calm the guests and help them enjoy their surroundings. Some Japanese houses even have a special 'tea room'.

The surroundings for the tea ceremony are important. There is usually a scroll on the wall and a vase of flowers. These would have been specially chosen for the occasion. Tea ceremonies might be held to celebrate the blossoming of the cherry trees in spring, or a get-together of friends.

A tea master serving t

Guests kneel on a mat called a 'tatami' (said tah-*tar*-me). They are served by the 'tea master', who has studied how to conduct tea ceremonies. The tea master uses a scoop to put some powdered green tea into the tea bowl. Hot water is ladled in. The tea is whisked, which makes it frothy. Sweets are served with the tea, because green tea can taste bitter.

Celebrations

New Year is an important time in many cultures. The date on which it is celebrated varies from culture to culture. Christmas customs and traditions also vary a lot from culture to culture.

New Year in Scotland

In Scotland, people celebrate the coming of the new year with a big party on New Year's Eve, 31 December. Scots call this celebration 'Hogmanay'.

In order to receive good luck in the new year, the first person to enter a Scottish home after midnight must be a black-haired man. He brings with him a piece of coal for the fire, which symbolises warmth for the house in the coming year. He also has some traditional Scottish food, such as **black bun**, to represent plenty of food. And under his arm he carries something to drink. Everyone sings 'Auld Lang Syne' – a traditional Scottish song celebrating the importance of old friends.

This man is known as your 'first foot' because he's the first person to put his foot across your doorway in the new year.

Chinese 'couplet' sayings on red paper

The Chinese New Year Festival

New Year in Western cultures can be a lively celebration that lasts from New Year's Eve to New Year's Day, but the Chinese New Year **Festival** can last from five days to three weeks!

Decorations are an important part of Chinese New Year. People hang 'couplets' on walls and in doorways at home. These are good-luck sayings written on pieces of red paper.

Dinner on Chinese New Year's Eve is the most important meal of the year, because it's when the whole family gets together. The foods that are eaten are symbols of success and abundance for the following year. A whole fish or a whole chicken is considered lucky.

On New Year's Eve, family members give each other money in red envelopes. This is called 'lucky money', because it symbolises having money during the coming year.

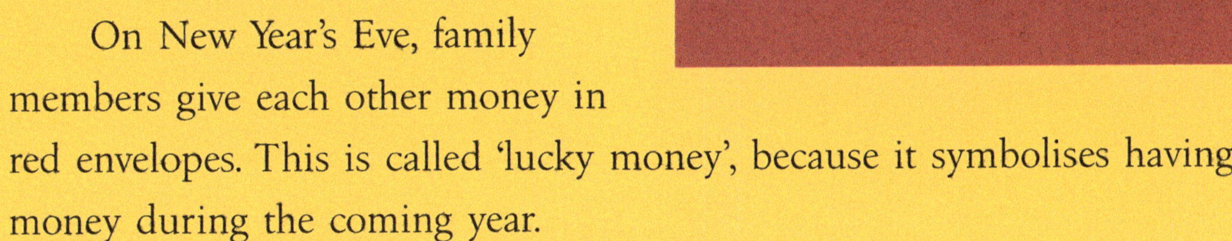

Did you know?

Chinese New Year begins at a different time every year. For example, in 2002, Chinese New Year started on 12 February, but in 2003 the date was 1 February.

A traditional panettone

An Italian Christmas

At Christmas time, Italians like to eat special foods such as 'panettone' (said pan-uh-*toe*-nay). These are cakes with sultanas and candied fruit inside them. One hundred years ago, traditional panettone were small and round and packed in drum-shaped boxes. Today, they are tall and packed in square-shaped boxes. The modern panettone boxes are now famous around the world.

In Italy, strolling musicians called 'zampognari' play traditional Christmas songs in the streets, using bagpipes, flutes and oboes.

Oh, Christmas Tree!

The tradition of having a decorated tree at Christmas began in Germany over 400 years ago. The first Christmas trees were a simple branch of a pine tree or a holly tree. They were decorated with paper roses and apples. Many years later, people used candles to give light to the tree. Gradually, the tradition of having a Christmas tree spread to other parts of Europe, and to the United States. Queen Victoria's husband, who was born in Germany, was the first person to set up a Christmas tree in England, at Windsor Castle in 1841.

A German Christmas carol called 'O Tannenbaum' ('O Christmas Tree') celebrates the delight of having a living green tree in the home at Christmas, when many trees in the northern hemisphere are so bare without their leaves.

Thanksgiving Day

Thanksgiving is an American celebration that is centuries old. It began when the pilgrims gave thanks for the harvest and for having enough food to survive the upcoming winter.

The original Thanksgiving included the Native Americans who had helped the pilgrims settle and raise crops.

The traditional Thanksgiving meal includes turkey, stuffing, sweet potatoes, and pumpkin pie for dessert.

Did you know?

Thanksgiving Day in the United States is held on the fourth Thursday in November, whereas in Canada people celebrate on the second Monday in October.

National Dress

kilts

Throughout the world, there are many cultures that have a traditional dress, or costume. There is the bold tartan kilt in Scotland, the richly-coloured sari in India and the beautiful sarong in Indonesia.

Different kinds of clothing were produced to suit different climates, and they were made of materials that were easily obtained.

sari

sarongs

The Scottish kilt

The kilt is like a skirt. The first kilts were much bigger than those worn today, and could be taken off and used as a blanket at night. It must have been very handy in cold Scottish winters!

Today kilts in Scotland are mainly kept for special occasions like weddings and traditional celebrations. There are up to eight metres of material in every kilt, making them quite heavy to wear.

The Japanese kimono

The word 'kimono' is Japanese for 'a thing to wear'. It is a long, loose piece of clothing with wide sleeves. It is tied with a wide sash, or belt, called an 'obi'. Kimonos don't have pockets, so a small wooden box, called an 'inro', can be attached to the obi and used to carry things.

Today, Japanese women wear the kimono for special occasions such as **graduations** or weddings, or for traditional ceremonies.

Fun and Games

Today, children who live in cultures with modern technology can play games on computers. Hand-held electronic games are also popular. Like computers, they have silicon chips inside them to make them work.

In the past, children played simple games, often using materials that they could find easily around them.

Knucklebones was a game that was played in Italy. It was played with small round pebbles. The game was called knucklebones because you had to throw the pebbles in the air, and catch them on the back of your hand, on your knuckles.

jacks

The same game was also played in Australia and Britain, where children called it jacks. As time passed, the jacks were made from brightly coloured plastic, and were all exactly the same shape.

Another game played in many different cultures was bowling a hoop. Old-fashioned hoops were made of steel or wood. Today hoops are plastic. Some children like swinging them around their waist.

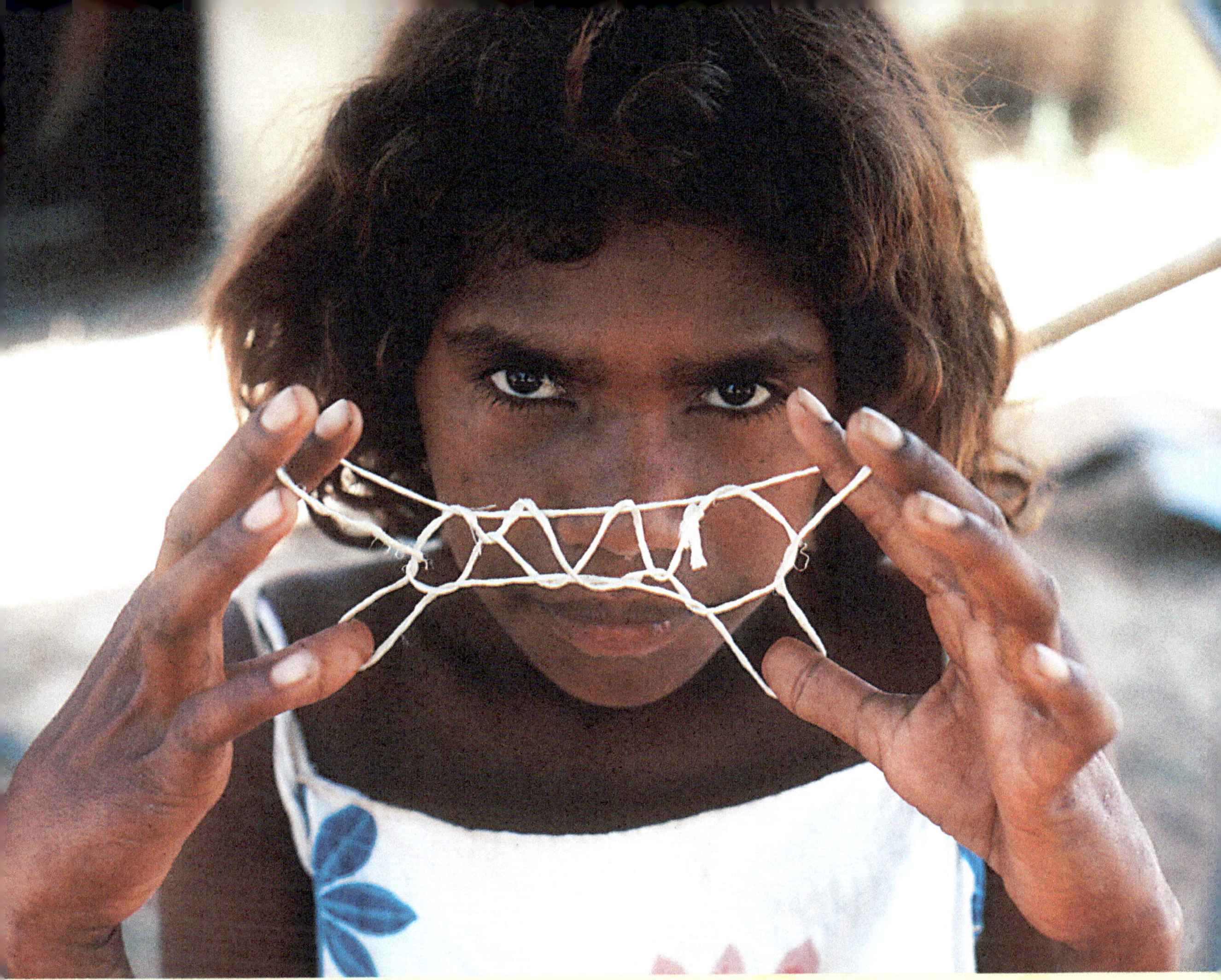

Aboriginal children's games

Aboriginal children living in the Australian bush also had to make up games using materials they could find.

A popular game was the string game. Children used string that was made from the bark of trees, or the leaves of plants. They tied the string in a circle, and used the fingers on both hands to form patterns.

A series of patterns was used to tell myths. The skill of making the patterns, and telling the stories, was passed from parent to child.

CHAPTER 6

Language

Words and language are an important part of any culture. People use language to communicate with each other. Even when people speak the same language, such as English, they use words differently, depending on where they live.

Proverbs and sayings can reveal a lot about a culture. 'He who hesitates is lost' is an Australian proverb. 'To a quick question, give a slow answer' is an Italian proverb. So in Australian culture, people seem to think it's best to act quickly, whereas in the Italian culture the opposite is thought to be better.

Even when a proverb means the same thing, it may consist of different words. For example, to avoid bad luck, Americans say 'knock on wood', whereas Australians say 'touch wood' and Italians say 'touch iron'!

Did you know?

'Universal signs' like these three are understood by everyone. That is very handy when you are travelling and need to find the toilets!

Language links

Different cultures take words from other languages. 'Anorak' is an Eskimo word for a short coat with a hood that protects you from wind, rain or cold. 'Parka' is another Eskimo word that was used to describe an anorak with a fur-lined hood.

'Anorak' and 'parka' were originally Eskimo words.

English-speakers use the French word 'gourmet' to describe someone who knows a lot about food.

Another word used in English is 'pow-wow' – meaning 'to get together for a chat, or discussion'. It comes from a similar-sounding word used by some Native American tribes.

Did you know?

Over 3000 languages will disappear this century as many cultures stop speaking their own language and use English, or Chinese, instead.

'Kiosk' is often used to describe a small shop that is open at the front, and sells newspapers, sandwiches and drinks. It comes from the Turkish word for 'a pavilion', which is 'kiusk'.

The word 'kiosk' comes from Turkey.

Symbols

The symbols of a country are usually its flag, a **coat of arms** and **emblems** such as plants or animals.

Flags

The first flags were designed hundreds of years ago. Flags are used to represent a country, and unite the many cultures living there. Some flags are designed to reflect the history of a country. For example, the flag of the United States of America has 50 stars representing the number of states today. It also has 13 red and white stripes, which stand for the original states from which the country grew.

At the opening ceremony the Olympic Games, teams fr different countries are led by th flag-bearer. Although a flag a simple rectangle of colour cloth, at an international event becomes a powerful symbol of country or national team.

American flag

Did you know?

Some national flags are the result of a design competition. There were more than 30,000 entries in the competition to design the present Australian flag!

Australia also has an Aboriginal flag.

Coats of arms

A coat of arms is a cultural symbol that is used by governments on buildings, and in official documents like passports.

On the American coat of arms, the American bald eagle is carrying a scroll with the motto 'E Pluribus Unum'. These Latin words mean 'Out of many, one', because America, like many countries today, was formed from several cultures living in the one place.

The Australian coat of arms features an emu and a kangaroo.

National emblems

Native plants or animals are often used as the symbols, or emblems, of a country.

Canada

maple leaf

beaver

New Zealand

silver fern

kiwi

Scotland

thistle

England

rose

Australia

golden wattle

CHAPTER 8

Music and Dance

Music and dancing are an important part of many cultures. Some Aborigines in Australia still perform ceremonial dances called corroborees. These dances are a tradition passed down from one generation to another.

Did you know?

While the men dance at a corroboree, the women drum out the rhythm, beating with sticks on animal skins they have stretched tightly across their legs. Sometimes the women also sing.

Corroborees are held at night, by the light of a fire – or by moonlight.

Maori haka

A 'haka' is a traditional Maori dance. The New Zealand rugby team, the All Blacks, and the Maori team (shown below), sometimes perform a haka before playing a match.

Almost every part of the body is used in a haka. It is a complicated dance, where the eyes, tongue and the muscles of the face twist into different expressions. The dancers chant words as their arms and legs perform the movements.

Did you know?

In Maori tradition, different kinds of haka are used to entertain, or welcome, special guests. Maori women sit and sing while Maori men dance.

CHAPTER 9

Culture on the Move

When people migrate from one country to another, they sometimes continue doing the things they enjoyed doing in the country or culture from which they came. An example of this is the Italian game, bocce.

Bocce (said bott-shay) is an ancient game that probably began in Egypt and spread to the Roman Empire. It is like an Italian form of bowls, but is played outdoors. There are eight wooden bocce balls that are shared between two teams. The balls are different colours so that each team can recognise its own balls after they are bowled onto the court. As well, there is a third, differently coloured, ball called the 'pallino'. Each team aims to get closest to the pallino when it bowls its balls onto the court.

These Italian migrants, living in Australia, are playing bocce. They used to play this game back in Italy. When they first played bocce in their new country, they played for fun in backyards, streets or the local park. Now the sport is so popular in Australia that there are many bocce clubs and organised competitions.

Oral history

Migrants in many countries are now taking part in **oral history** projects, in which they are interviewed about their memories of the past. They describe their old culture, and the challenges of settling into a new culture. Oral history is an important way of recording migrants' experiences when they move from one country to another.

Maria Donato's family

Maria Donato was born in 1915 in a village in Italy. She arrived in Australia in 1933.

Interviewer: *What was it like at home in Ascoli Piceno?*

Maria: *We lived near a river. I would get round pebbles from the river and play knucklebones with them. I used to knit socks for the boys, help do the washing by hand and make wine with my Dad.*

Interviewer: *What sorts of food did you have?*

Maria: *My Mum and I used to make the bread. We had our own fowls, eggs, rabbits for eating, a vegetable garden and a vineyard. We made our own sausages, and stored them for the cold winter months. We didn't have a refrigerator or ice-chest. To keep meat cool we put it in a bag and put it down the well.*

Interviewer: *What did you learn about at school?*

Maria: *Our teacher would read to us from the newspaper. She read about Marconi's invention of the wireless. I had to leave school when I was ten, after which I learned dressmaking.*

Interviewer: *Did you have a radio ever at home?*

Maria: *We never had a radio. We listened to the news in the village where the men used to talk about politics.*

Interviewer: *What about friends?*

Maria: *All my friends were special. They were like members of my family. There was dancing when the farmers finished the harvest. There was food too; ravioli, torte and other sweets. Everyone went.*

Interviewer: *When did you come to Australia and why did you come?*

Maria: *When I was about ten, Dad went to live in Australia because he thought the climate would be better for his health. Dad worked so Mum and my brothers could join him. It took eight years before I saw him again. I remember his address because I was always writing to him.*

CHAPTER 10

Change in Time

Almost every culture in the world is changing today. The greatest changes have been brought about by the effects of new technology.

Modern transport has changed many cultures. Cars, buses and trains have often replaced walking, riding horses and cycling. People can now travel great distances in much less time.

Computers have made life very different from 100 years ago. People can travel the world on the internet and email news to friends and family in distant countries at the touch of a button.

As technology allows people around the world to mix more and more, cultures will continue to change.

Glossary

Black bun	A pie-like Scottish dessert. It is so full of raisins and currants that it looks black.
Ceremony	An occasion such as a tea ceremony, wedding or graduation, when traditional activities are carried out.
Coat of arms	An emblem or symbol that represents a country, city or family. It sometimes has a motto.
Emblem	A symbol.
Festival	A fun time when people get together to celebrate something such as a harvest, a kind of music, or an event in the past.
Graduation	A ceremony when someone gets their university degree or special qualification.
Migrate	To move from one country to another to live.
Oral history	History passed down by word of mouth, often in an interview.
Proverb	An old saying, giving advice to others.
Tucker	An informal, or casual, word for everyday food.
Virtual traveller	A person who learns about other countries using the Internet. They can feel as though they are visiting another country.